ISBN 978-1-70513-457-3

Cover photo © Pictorial Press Ltd / Alamy Stock Photo

**HAL•LEONARD®**

Visit Hal Leonard Online at
**www.halleonard.com**

Contact us:
**Hal Leonard**
7777 West Bluemound Road
Milwaukee, WI 53213
Email: info@halleonard.com

In Europe, contact:
**Hal Leonard Europe Limited**
42 Wigmore Street
Marylebone, London, W1U 2RN
Email: info@halleonardeurope.com

In Australia, contact:
**Hal Leonard Australia Pty. Ltd.**
4 Lentara Court
Cheltenham, Victoria, 3192 Australia
Email: info@halleonard.com.au

# Welcome to the *Super Easy Songbook* series!

## This unique collection will help you play your favorite songs quickly and easily. Here's how it works:

- Play the simplified melody with your right hand. Letter names appear inside each note to assist you.

- There are no key signatures to worry about! If a sharp ♯ or flat ♭ is needed, it is shown beside the note each time.

- There are no page turns, so your hands never have to leave the keyboard.

- If two notes are connected by a tie ‿, hold the first note for the combined number of beats. (The second note does not show a letter name since it is not re-struck.)

- Add basic chords with your left hand using the provided keyboard diagrams. Chord voicings have been carefully chosen to minimize hand movement.

- The left-hand rhythm is up to you, and chord notes can be played together or separately. Be creative!

- If the chords sound muddy, move your left hand an octave* higher. If this gets in the way of playing the melody, move your right hand an octave higher as well.

  * *An octave spans eight notes. If your starting note is C, the next C to the right is an octave higher.*

—————————————— ALSO AVAILABLE ——————————————

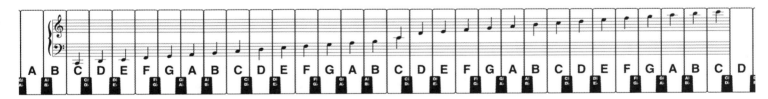

Hal Leonard Student Keyboard Guide HL00296039

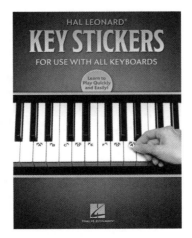

Key Stickers HL00100016

# All Along the Watchtower

# Blowin' in the Wind

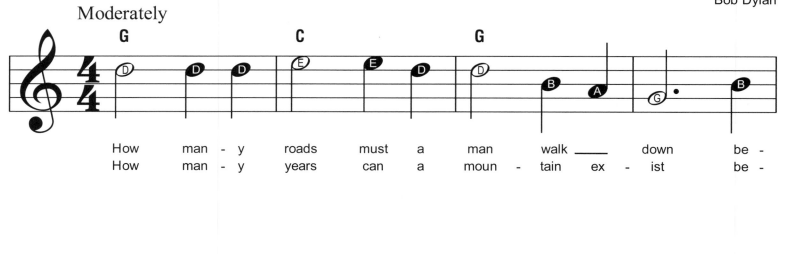

Words and Music by
Bob Dylan

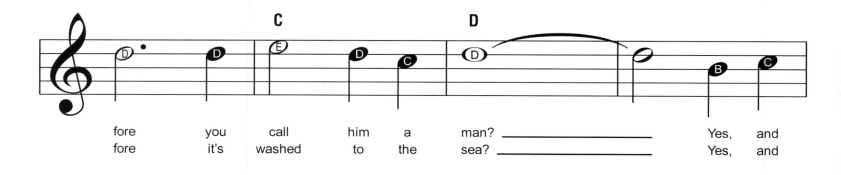

How man-y roads must a man walk _____ down be -
How man-y years can a moun-tain ex - ist be -

fore you call him a man? _____ Yes, and
fore it's washed him to the sea? _____ Yes, and

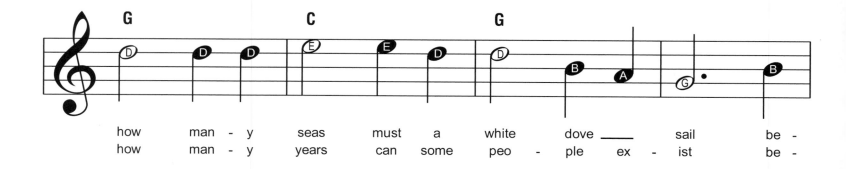

how man-y seas must a white dove _____ sail be -
how man-y years can some white peo - ple ex - ist be -

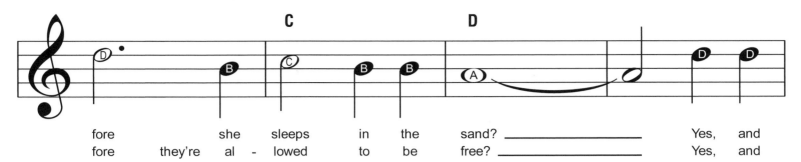

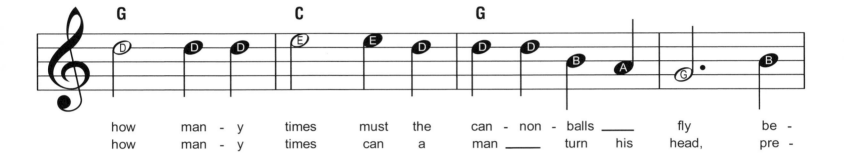

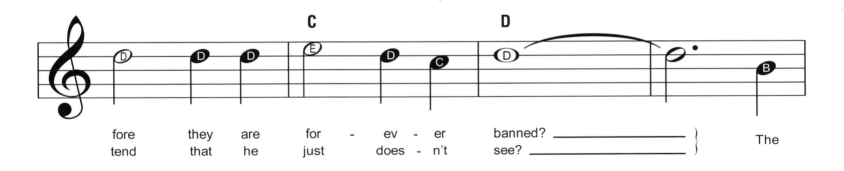

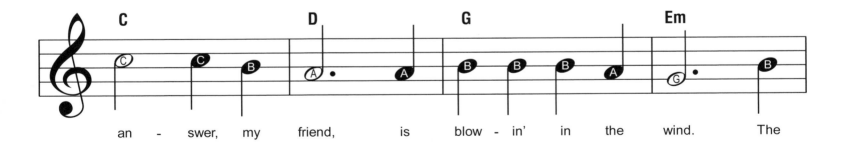

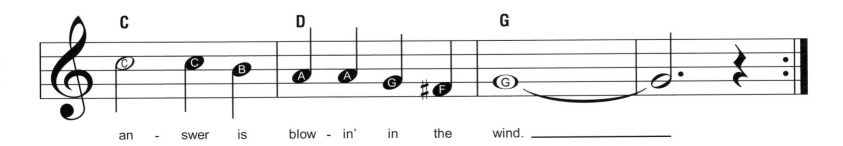

# Don't Think Twice, It's All Right

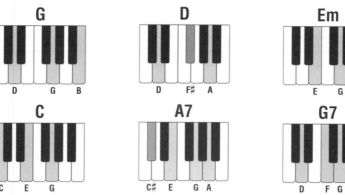

Words and Music by
Bob Dylan

Moderate half-time feel

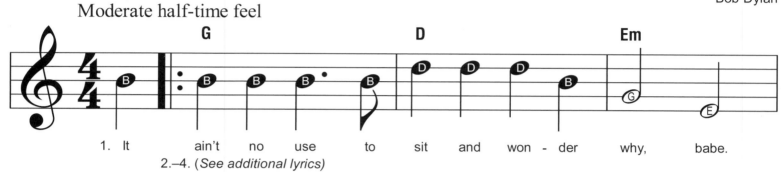

1. It ain't no use to sit and won - der why, babe.
2.–4. (*See additional lyrics*)

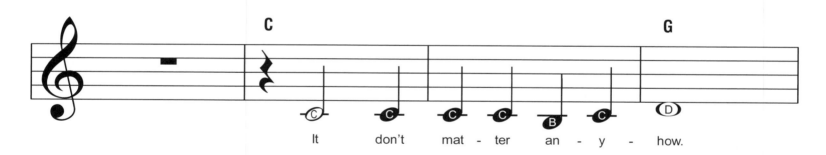

It don't mat - ter an - y - how.

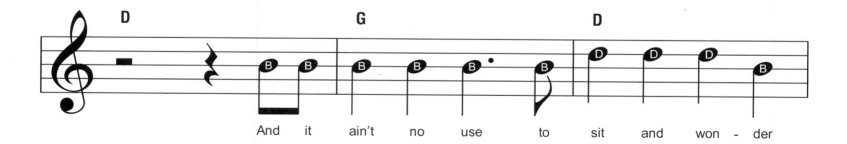

And it ain't no use to sit and won - der

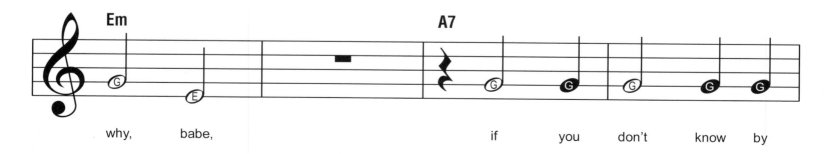

why, babe, if you don't know by

*Additional Lyrics*

2. It ain't no use in turnin' on your light, babe.
   That light I never knowed.
   And it ain't no use in turnin' on your light, babe.
   I'm on the dark side of the road.
   Still, I wish there was somethin' you would do or say
   To try and make me change my mind and stay.
   We never did too much talkin' anyway.
   So don't think twice, it's all right.

3. It ain't no use in callin' out my name, gal,
   Like you never did before.
   It ain't no use in callin' out my name, gal.
   I can't hear you anymore.
   I'm a-thinkin' and a-wond'rin' all the way down the road.
   I once loved a woman, a child, I'm told,
   I give her my heart, but she wanted my soul.
   But don't think twice, it's all right.

4. I'm walkin' down that long, lonesome road, babe.
   Where I'm bound, I can't tell.
   But goodbye's too good a word, gal,
   So I'll just say fare thee well.
   I ain't sayin' you treated me unkind.
   You could have done better, but I don't mind.
   You just kinda wasted my precious time.
   But don't think twice, it's all right.

# Forever Young

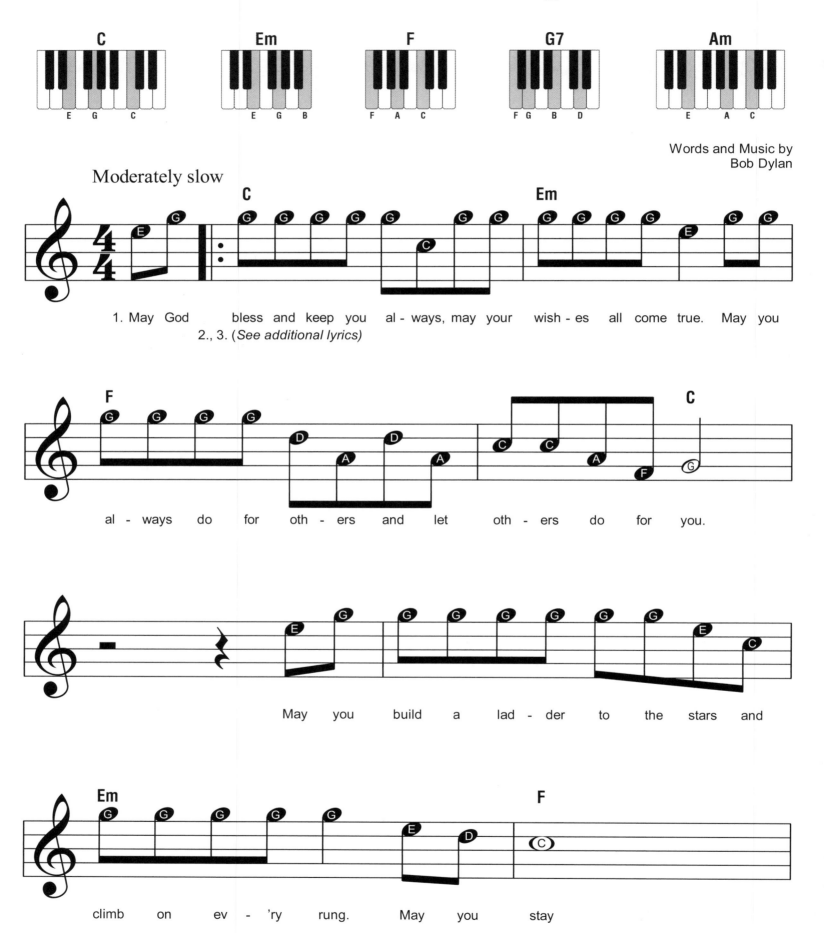

Words and Music by
Bob Dylan

1. May God bless and keep you al - ways, may your wish - es all come true. May you
2., 3. (*See additional lyrics*)

al - ways do for oth - ers and let oth - ers do for you.

May you build a lad - der to the stars and

climb on ev - 'ry rung. May you stay

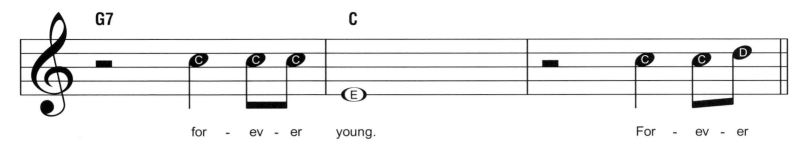

for - ev - er young. For - ev - er

Chorus

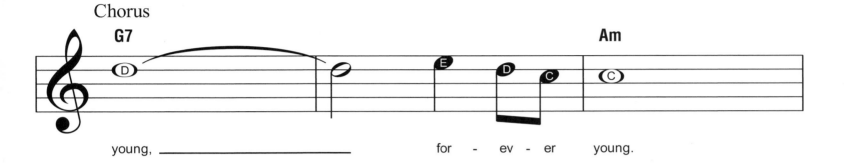

young, _____ for - ev - er young.

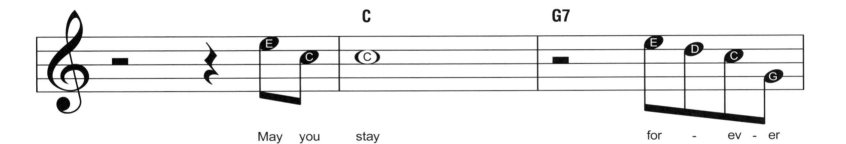

May you stay for - ev - er

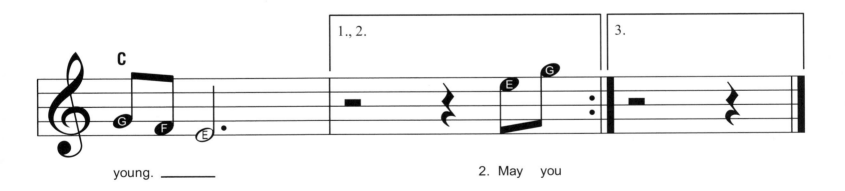

young. _____ 2. May you

*Additional Lyrics*

2. May you grow up to be righteous,
May you grow up to be true.
May you always know the truth
And see the lights surrounding you.
May you always be courageous,
Stand upright and be strong,
And may you stay forever young.
*(To Chorus)*

3. May your hands always be busy,
May your feet always be swift.
May you have a strong foundation
When the winds of changes shift.
May your heart always be joyful,
May your song always be sung,
And may you stay forever young.
*(To Chorus)*

# Hurricane

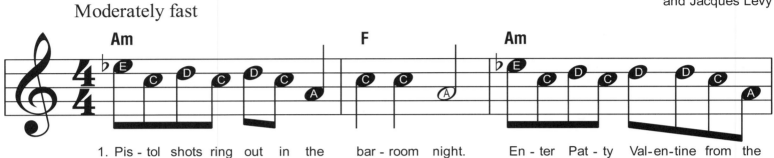

Words and Music by Bob Dylan
and Jacques Levy

Moderately fast

1. Pis - tol shots ring out in the bar - room night. En - ter Pat - ty Val - en - tine from the

2.–11. (*See additional lyrics*)

up - per hall. She sees the bar - tend - er in a pool of blood,

cries out, "My God, they killed them all!" Here comes the sto - ry of the

Hur - ri - cane, the man the au - thor - i - ties came to blame

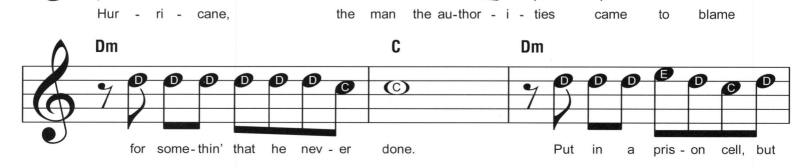

for some - thin' that he nev - er done. Put in a pris - on cell, but

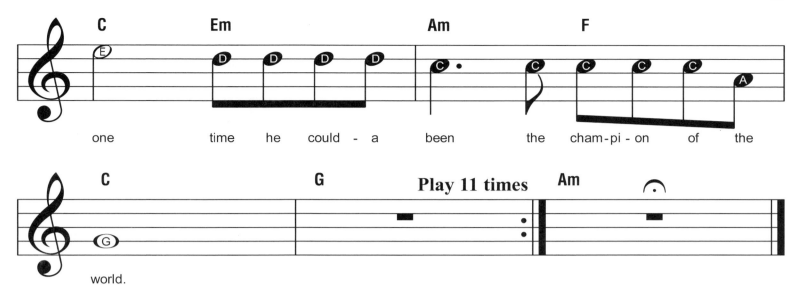

one time he could - a been the cham-pi - on of the

world.

*Additional Lyrics*

2. Three bodies lyin' there does Patty see,
And another man named Bello, movin' around mysteriously.
"I didn't do it," he says, and he throws up his hands.
"I was only robbin' the register, I hope you understand.
I saw them leavin'," he says, and he stops.
"One of us had better call up the cops."
And so Patty calls the cops,
And they arrive on the scene with their red lights flashin'
In the hot New Jersey night.

3. Meanwhile, far away in another part of town,
Rubin Carter and a couple of friends are drivin' around.
Number one contender for the middleweight crown,
Had no idea what kinda shit was about to go down
When a cop pulled him over to the side of the road,
Just like the time before and the time before that.
In Paterson that's just the way things go.
If you're black, you might as well not show up on the street,
'Less you wanna draw the heat.

4. Alfred Bello had a partner and he had a rap for the cops.
Him and Arthur Dexter Bradley were just out prowlin' around.
He said, "I saw two men runnin' out, they looked like middleweights.
They jumped into a white car with out-of-state plates."
And Miss Patty Valentine just nodded her head.
Cop said, "Wait a minute, boys, this one's not dead."
So they took him to the infirmary,
And though this man could hardly see,
They told him that he could identify the guilty men.

5. Four in the mornin' and they haul Rubin in,
They take him to the hospital and they bring him upstairs.
The wounded man looks up through his one dyin' eye,
Says, "Wha'd you bring him in here for? He ain't the guy!"
Yes, here's the story of the Hurricane,
The man the authorities came to blame
For somethin' that he never done.
Put in a prison cell, but one time he could-a been
The champion of the world.

6. Four months later, the ghettos are in flame.
Rubin's in South America, fightin' for his name,
While Arthur Dexter Bradley's still in the robbery game.
And the cops are puttin' the screws to him,
 lookin' for somebody to blame.
"Remember that murder that happened in a bar?"
"Remember you said you saw the getaway car?"
"You think you'd like to play ball with the law?"
"Think it might-a been that fighter that you saw runnin' that night?"
"Don't forget that you are white."

7. Arthur Dexter Bradley said, "I'm really not sure."
Cops said, "A poor boy like you could use a break.
We got you for the motel job and we're talkin' to your friend Bello.
Now, you don't wanna have to go back to jail; be a nice fellow.
You'll be doin' society a favor.
That son-of-a-bitch is brave and gettin' braver.
We want to put his ass in stir.
We want to pin this triple murder on him.
He ain't no Gentleman Jim."

8. Rubin could take a man out with just one punch,
But he never did like to talk about it all that much.
"It's my work," he'd say, and I do it for pay,
"And when it's over I'd just as soon go on my way
Up to some paradise
Where the trout streams flow and the air is nice,
And ride a horse along a trail."
But then they took him to the jailhouse
Where they try to turn a man into a mouse.

9. All of Rubin's cards were marked in advance.
The trial was a pig-circus; he never had a chance.
The judge made Rubin's witnesses drunkards from the slums.
To the white folks who watched, he was a revolutionary bum.
And to the black folks, he was just a crazy n****r.
No one doubted that he pulled the trigger.
And though they could not produce the gun,
The D.A. said he was the one who did the deed,
And the all-white jury agreed.

10. Rubin Carter was falsely tried.
The crime was murder one; guess who testified?
Bello and Bradley, and they both baldly lied.
And the newspapers, they all went along for the ride.
How can the life of such a man
Be in the palm of some fool's hand?
To see him obviously framed
Couldn't help but make me feel ashamed to live in a land
Where justice is a game.

11. Now all the criminals in their coats and their ties
Are free to drink martinis and watch the sun rise,
While Rubin sits like Buddha in a ten-foot cell,
An innocent man in a living hell.
Yes, that's the story of the Hurricane,
But it won't be over till they clear his name
And give him back the time he's done.
Put in a prison cell, but one time he could-a been
The champion of the world.

# I Shall Be Released

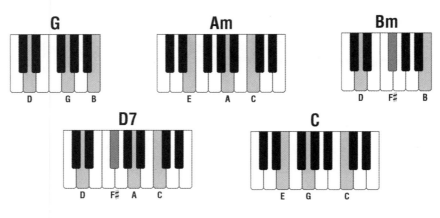

Words and Music by
Bob Dylan

Moderately bright

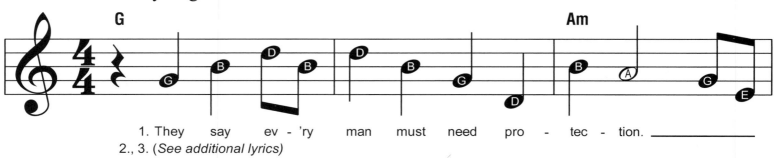

1. They say ev - 'ry man must need pro - tec - tion. _____
2., 3. (*See additional lyrics*)

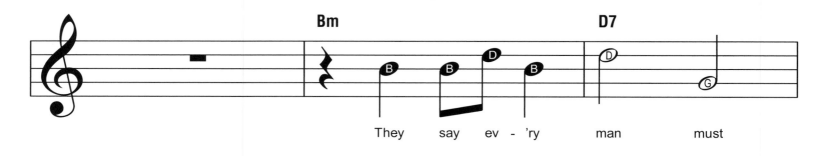

They say ev - 'ry man must

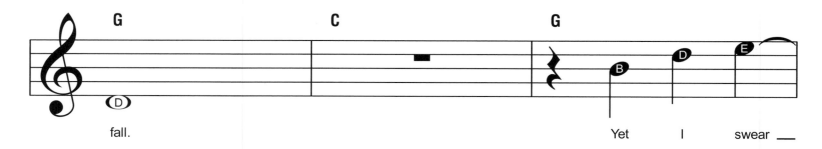

fall. Yet I swear ___

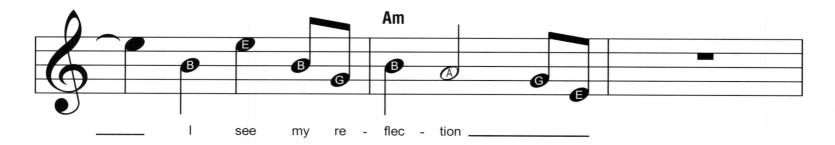

_____ I see my re - flec - tion _____

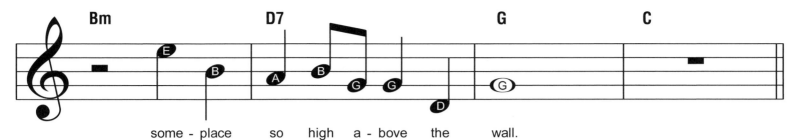

some - place    so    high  a - bove    the    wall.

Chorus

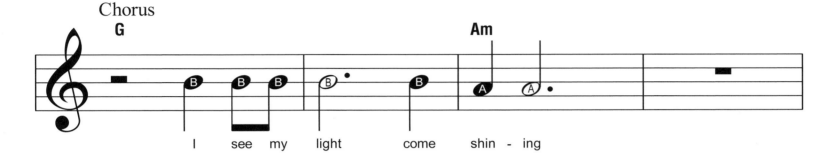

I    see    my    light    come    shin - ing

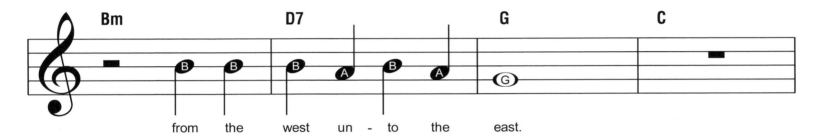

from    the    west    un - to    the    east.

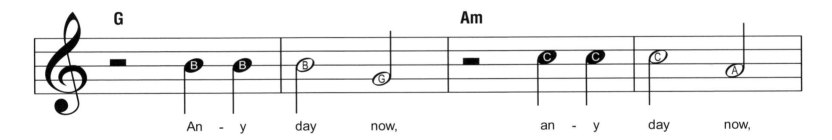

An - y    day    now,    an - y    day    now,

**Play 3 times**

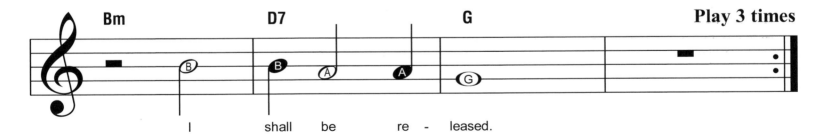

I    shall    be    re - leased.

*Additional Lyrics*

2. They say everything can be replaced,
Yet every distance is not near.
So I remember every face
Of every man who put me here.
*(To Chorus)*

3. Standing next to me in this lonely crowd
Is a man who swears he's not to blame.
All day long I hear him shout so loud,
Crying out that he was framed.
*(To Chorus)*

# I Want You

Words and Music by
Bob Dylan

Bright half-time feel

The guilt-y un-der-tak-er sighs, the lone-some or-gan grind-er cries, the sil-ver sax-o-phones say I should re-fuse you. _____ The cracked bells and washed-out horns blow in-to my face with scorn, but it's

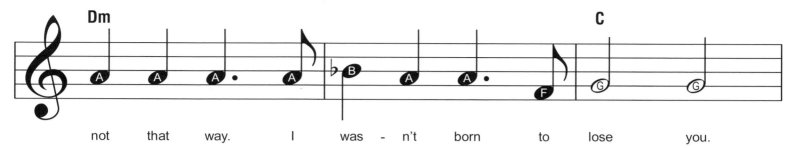

not that way. I was - n't born to lose you.

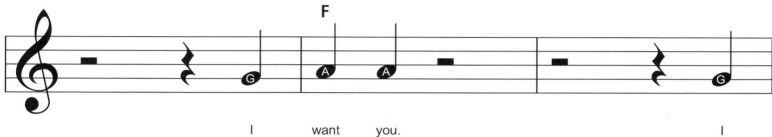

I want you. I

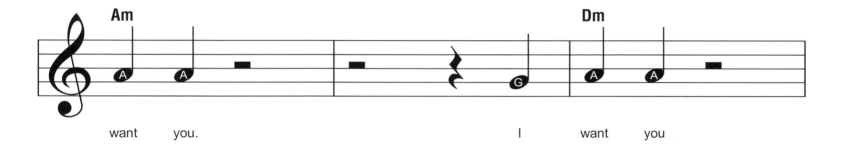

want you. I want you

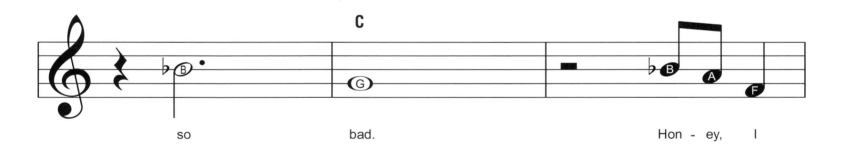

so bad. Hon - ey, I

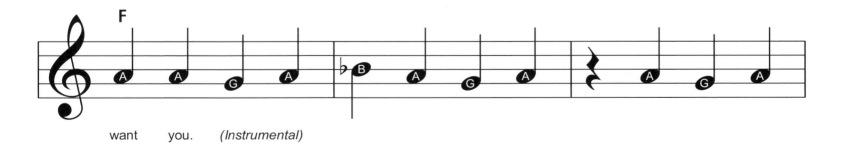

want you. *(Instrumental)*

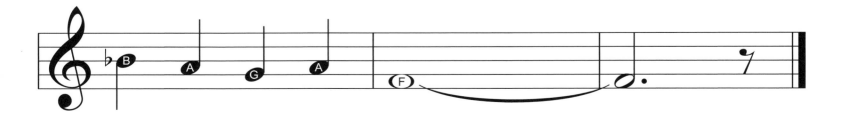

# It Ain't Me, Babe

Words and Music by
Bob Dylan

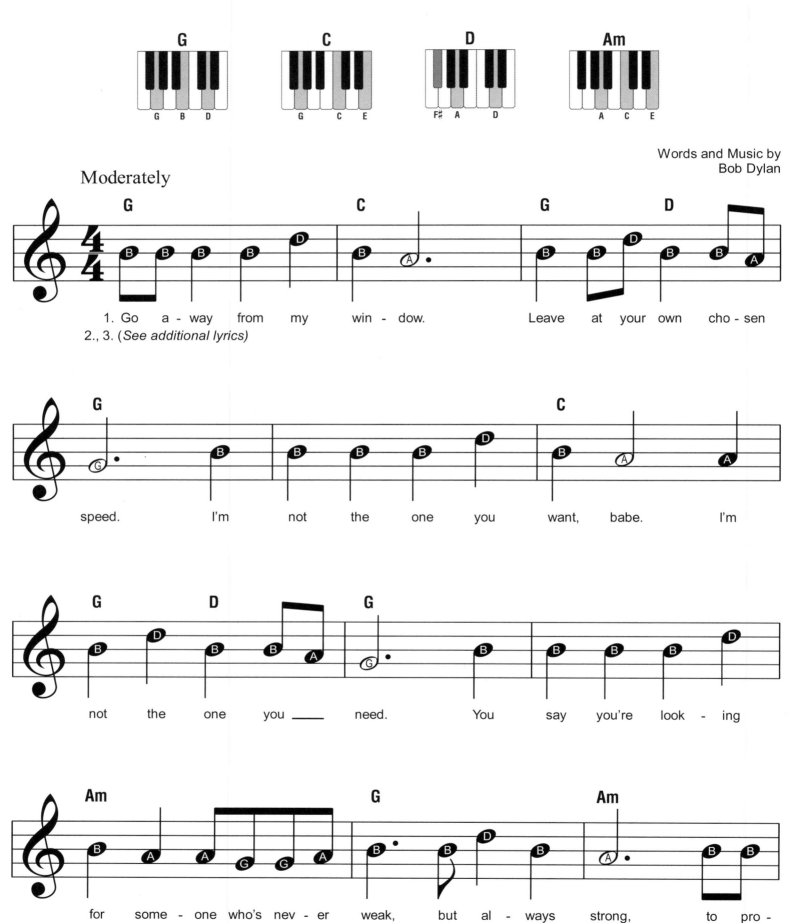

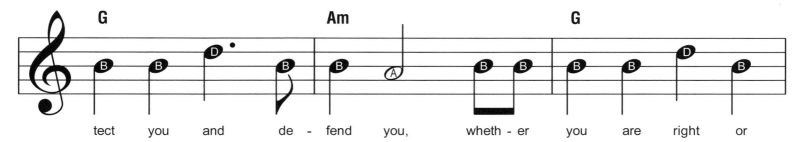

tect you and de - fend you, wheth - er you are right or

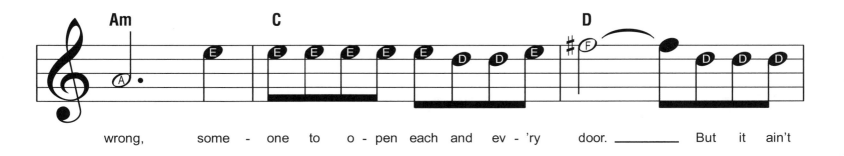

wrong, some - one to o - pen each and ev - 'ry door. _____ But it ain't

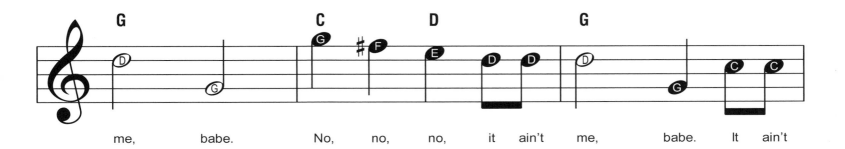

me, babe. No, no, no, it ain't me, babe. It ain't

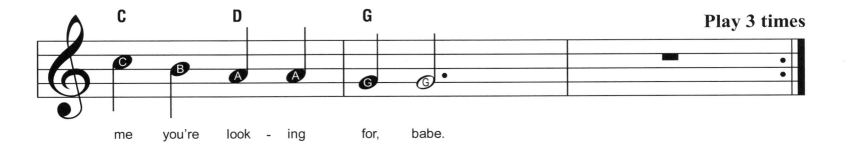

**Play 3 times**

me you're look - ing for, babe.

*Additional Lyrics*

2. Go lightly from the ledge, babe.
   Go lightly on the ground.
   I'm not the one you want, babe.
   I will only let you down.
   You say you're lookin' for someone
   Who will promise never to part.
   Someone to close his eyes for you,
   Someone to close his heart,
   Someone who will die for you and more.
   But it ain't me, babe.
   No, no, no, it ain't me, babe.
   It ain't me you're lookin' for, babe.

3. Go melt back in the night, babe.
   Everything inside is made of stone.
   There's nothing in here moving,
   And anyway, I'm not alone.
   You say you're lookin' for someone
   Who'll pick you up each time you fall,
   To gather flowers constantly
   And to come each time you call,
   A lover for your life and nothing more.
   But it ain't me, babe.
   No, no, no, it ain't me, babe.
   It ain't me you're lookin' for, babe.

# It's All Over Now, Baby Blue

Words and Music by
Bob Dylan

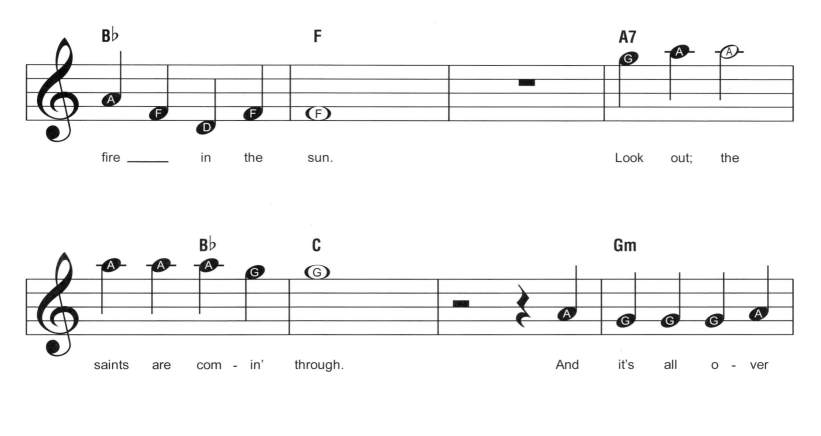

fire _____ in the sun. Look out; the

saints are com - in' through. And it's all o - ver

now, _____ Ba - by Blue. 2. The

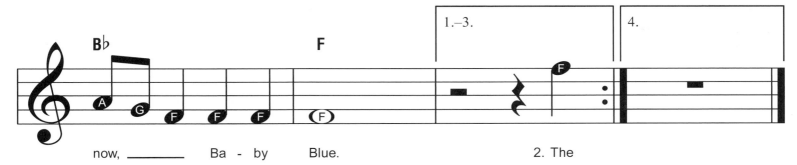

*Additional Lyrics*

2. The highway is for gamblers; better use your sense.
Take what you have gathered from coincidence.
The empty-handed painter from your streets
Is drawing crazy patterns on your sheets.
The sky, too, is folding under you.
And it's all over now, Baby Blue.

3. All your seasick sailors, they are rowing home.
All your reindeer armies are all going home.
Your lover who just walked out the door
Has taken all his blankets from the floor.
The carpet, too, is moving under you.
And it's all over now, Baby Blue.

4. Leave your stepping stones behind; now something calls for you.
Forget the dead you've left; they will not follow you.
The vagabond who's rapping at your door
Is standing in the clothes that you once wore.
Strike another match, go start anew.
And it's all over now, Baby Blue.

# Just Like a Woman

# Knockin' on Heaven's Door

Words and Music by
Bob Dylan

knock - in' on heav - en's door. _____
knock - in' on heav - en's door. _____

Knock, knock, knock - in' on heav - en's door.

Knock, knock, knock - in' on heav - en's door. _____

Knock, knock, knock - in' on heav - en's

door.

Knock, knock,

knock - in' on heav - en's door. _____

# Lay, Lady, Lay

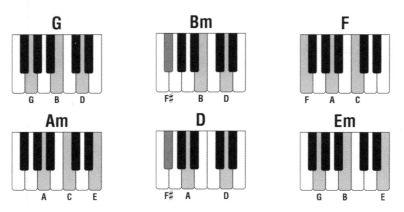

Words and Music by
Bob Dylan

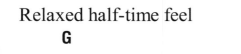
Relaxed half-time feel

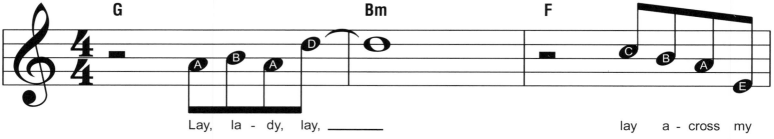

Lay, la - dy, lay, _____ lay a - cross my

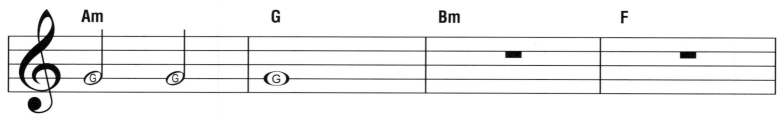

big brass bed.

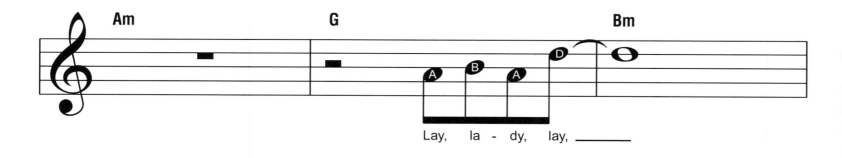

Lay, la - dy, lay, _____

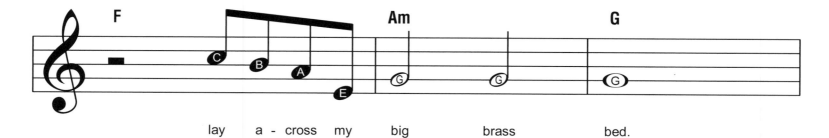

lay a - cross my big brass bed.

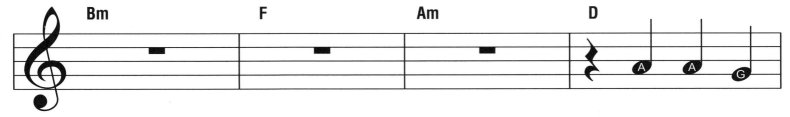

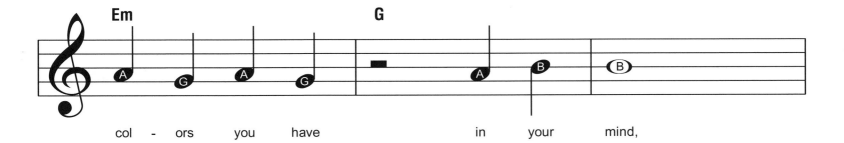

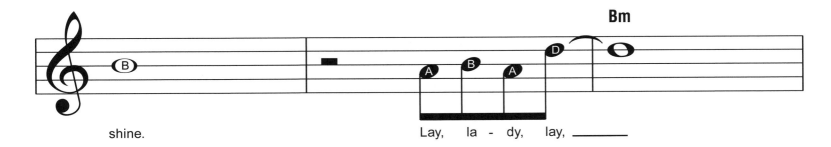

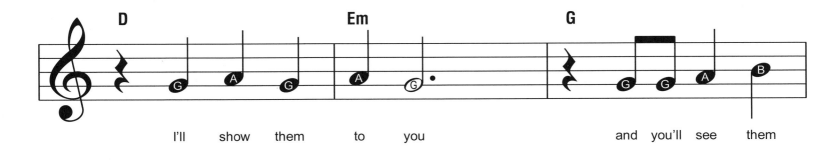

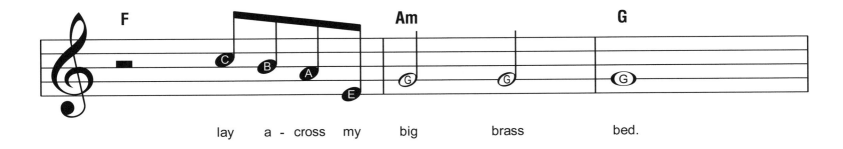

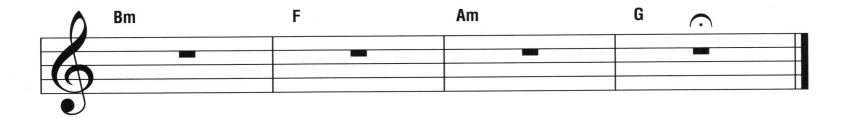

# Like a Rolling Stone

Words and Music by
Bob Dylan

# Maggie's Farm

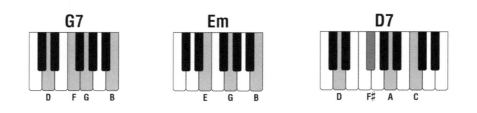

Words and Music by
Bob Dylan

Moderate half-time feel

1. I ain't gon - na work on Mag - gie's farm no more. ___
2.–5. (*See additional lyrics*)

___ No, I ain't gon - na work on Mag - gie's

farm no more. _____ Well, I wake up in the

morn - ing, fold my hands and pray for rain. _____ I got a

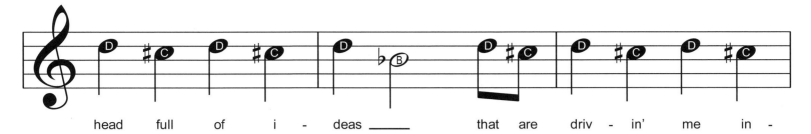

head full of i - deas _____ that are driv - in' me in -

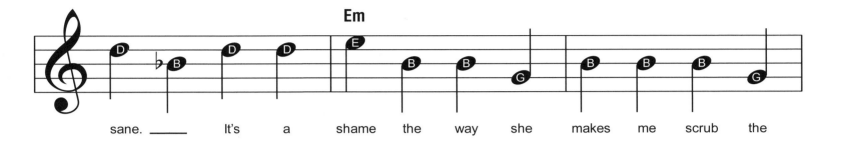

**Em**

sane. _____ It's a shame the way she makes me scrub the

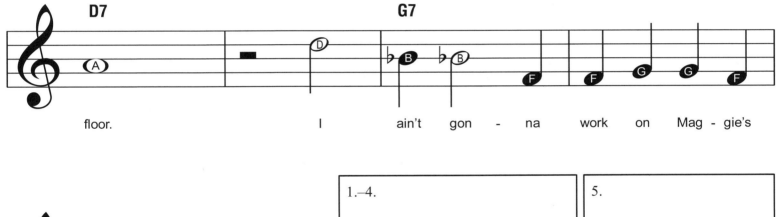

**D7**      **G7**

floor.      I      ain't gon - na work on Mag - gie's

1.–4.      5.

farm no more. _____      2.–5. I      _____

*Additional Lyrics*

2. I ain't gonna work for Maggie's brother no more.
No, I ain't gonna work for Maggie's brother no more.
Well, he hands you a nickel, he hands you a dime.
He asks you with a grin if you're havin' a good time.
Then he fines you every time you slam the door.
I ain't gonna work for Maggie's brother no more.

3. I ain't gonna work for Maggie's pa no more.
No, I ain't gonna work for Maggie's pa no more.
Well, he puts his cigar out in your face, just for kicks.
His bedroom window, it is made out of bricks.
The National Guard stands around his door.
I ain't gonna work for Maggie's pa no more.

4. I ain't gonna work for Maggie's ma no more.
No, I ain't gonna work for Maggie's ma no more.
Well, she talks to all the servants about man and God and law.
Everybody says she's the brains behind pa.
She's sixty-eight, but she says she's fifty-four.
I ain't gonna work for Maggie's ma no more.

5. I ain't gonna work on Maggie's farm no more.
I ain't gonna work on Maggie's farm no more.
Well, I try my best to be just like I am,
But everybody wants you to be just like them.
They say, "Sing while you slave" and I just get bored.
I ain't gonna work on Maggie's farm no more.

# Make You Feel My Love

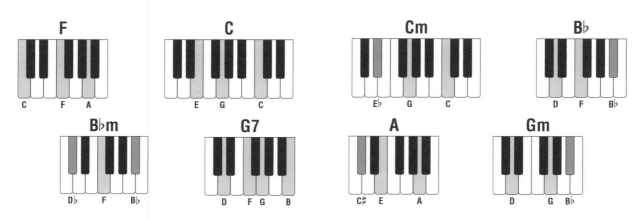

Words and Music by
Bob Dylan

Moderate Ballad

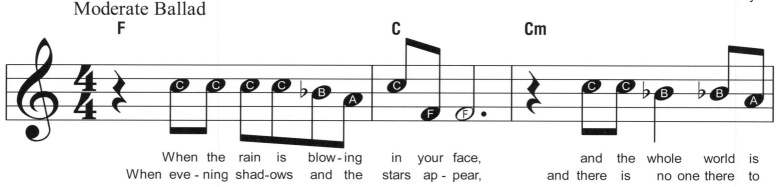

When the rain is blow-ing in your face, and the whole world is
When eve-ning shad-ows and the stars ap-pear, and there is no one there to

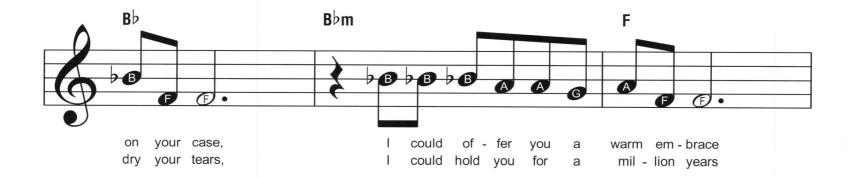

on your case, I could of-fer you a warm em-brace
dry your tears, I could hold you for a mil-lion years

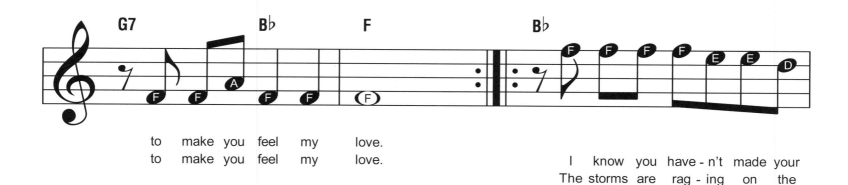

to make you feel my love.
to make you feel my love.
I know you have-n't made your
The storms are rag-ing on the

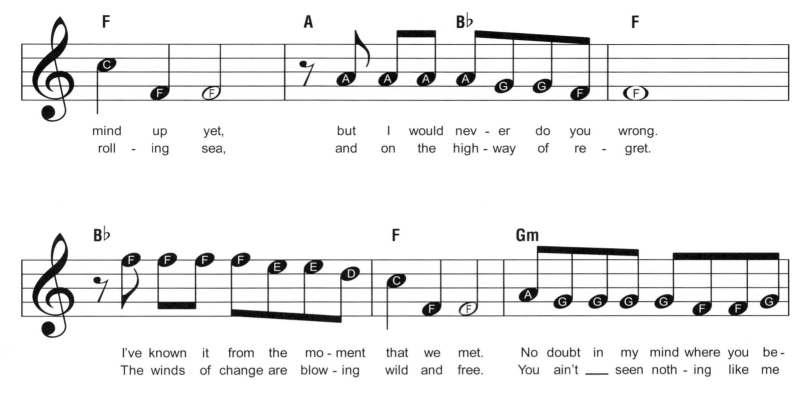

mind up yet, but I would nev - er do you wrong.
roll - ing sea, and on the high - way of re - gret.

I've known it from the mo - ment that we met. No doubt in my mind where you be -
The winds of change are blow - ing wild and free. You ain't ___ seen noth - ing like me

long.
yet. I'd go hun - gry, I'd go black and blue.
I could make you hap - py, make your dreams come true.

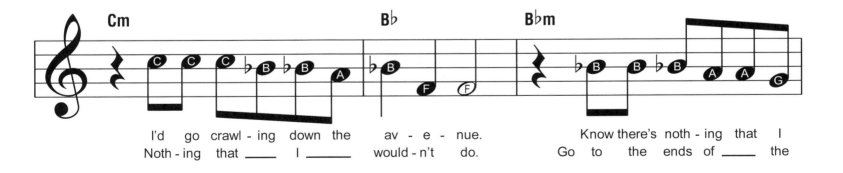

I'd go crawl - ing down the av - e - nue. Know there's noth - ing that I
Noth - ing that ___ I ___ would - n't do. Go to the ends of ___ the

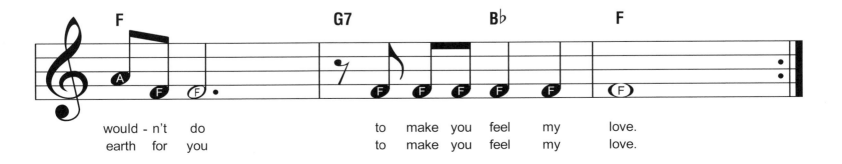

would - n't do to make you feel my love.
earth for you to make you feel my love.

# Mr. Tambourine Man

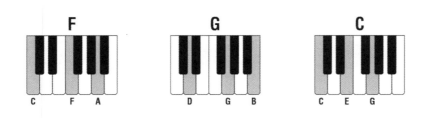

Words and Music by
Bob Dylan

Hey, Mis - ter Tam - bou - rine Man, play a song for

me. I'm not sleep - y and there is no place I'm go - in' to. ___

___ Hey, Mis - ter Tam - bou - rine Man, play a song for

**To Coda**

me. In the jin - gle jan - gle morn - in' I'll come fol - low - in'

# Positively 4th Street

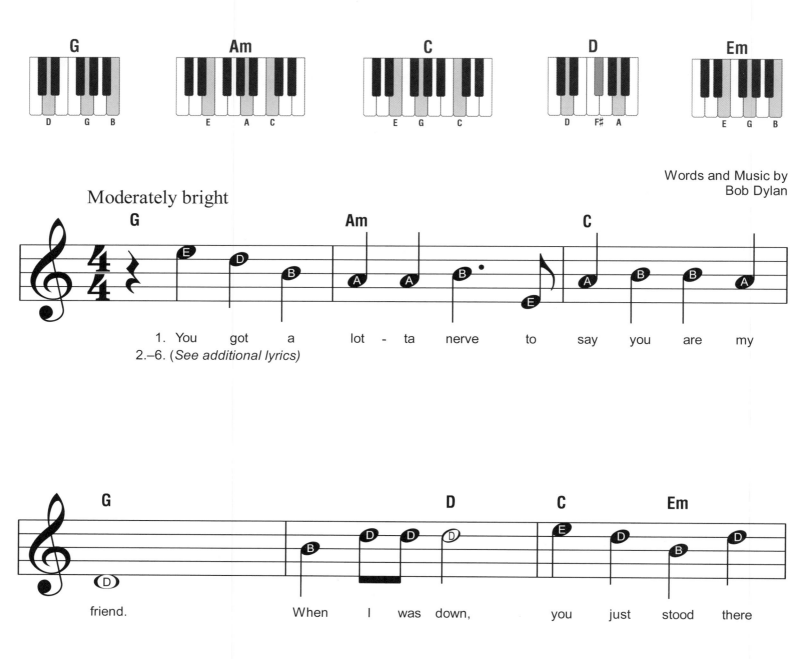

Words and Music by
Bob Dylan

Moderately bright

1. You got a lot-ta nerve to say you are my
2.–6. (*See additional lyrics*)

friend.    When I was down, you just stood there

grin - ning.    You got a

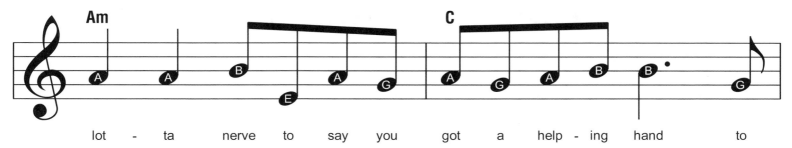

lot - ta nerve to say you got a help - ing hand to

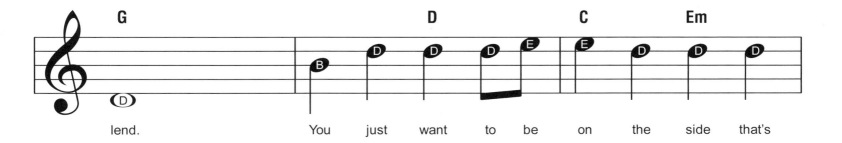

lend. You just want to be on the side that's

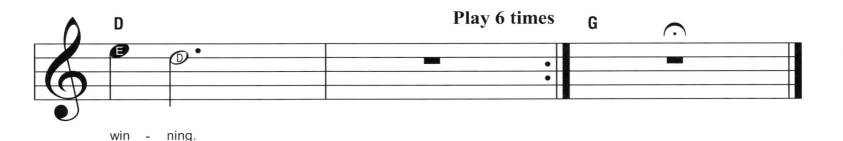

win - ning.

*Additional Lyrics*

2. You say I let you down; you know it's not like that.
   If you're so hurt, why then don't you show it?
   You say you've lost your faith, but that's not where it's at.
   You have no faith to lose, and you know it.

3. I know the reason that you talk behind my back.
   I used to be among the crowd you're in with.
   Do you take me for such a fool to think I'd make contact
   With the one who tries to hide what he don't know to begin with?

4. You see me on the street; you always act surprised.
   You say, "How are you? Good luck!" But you don't mean it.
   When you know as well as me you'd rather see me paralyzed,
   Why don't you just come out once and scream it?

5. No, I do not feel that good when I see the heartbreaks you embrace.
   If I was a master thief, perhaps I'd rob them.
   And now I know you're dissatisfied with your position and your place.
   Don't you understand it's not my problem?

6. I wish that for just one time you could stand inside my shoes,
   And just for that one moment I could be you.
   Yes, I wish that for just one time you could stand inside my shoes.
   You'd know what a drag it is to see you.

# Rainy Day Women #12 & 35

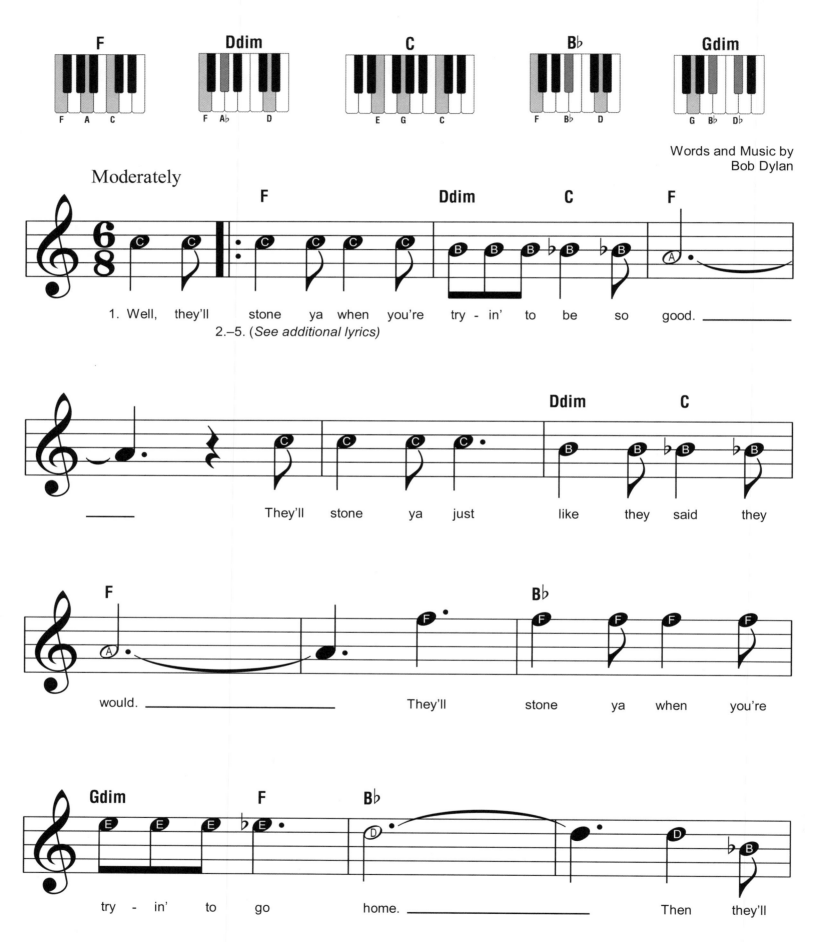

Words and Music by
Bob Dylan

Moderately

1. Well, they'll stone ya when you're try - in' to be so good. _____
2.–5. (*See additional lyrics*)

_____ They'll stone ya just like they said they

would. _____ They'll stone ya when you're

try - in' to go home. _____ Then they'll

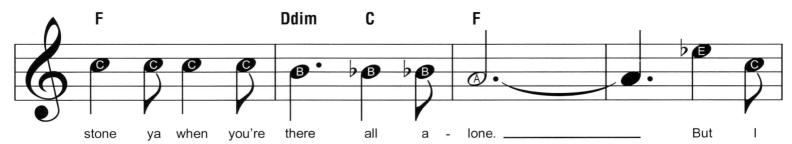

stone    ya    when    you're    there    all    a  -  lone. _____    But    I

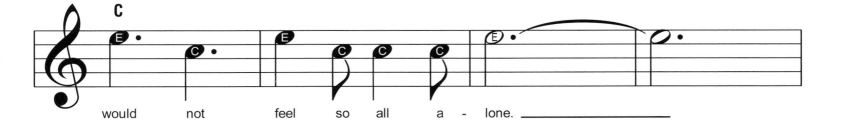

would    not    feel    so    all    a  -  lone. _____

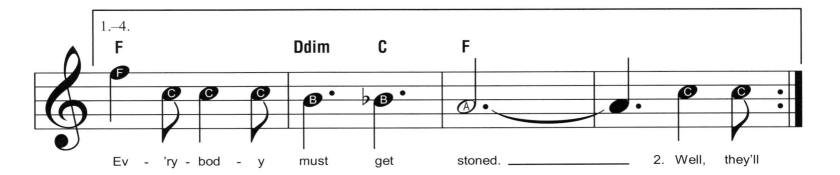

**1.–4.**

Ev  -  'ry  -  bod  -  y    must    get    stoned. _____    2. Well,    they'll

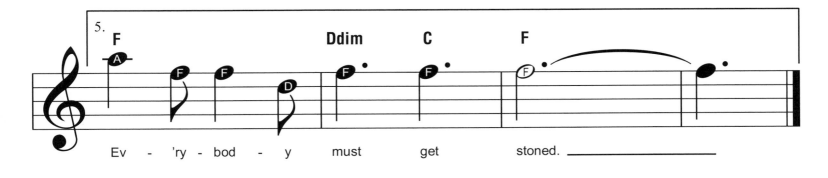

**5.**

Ev  -  'ry  -  bod  -  y    must    get    stoned. _____

*Additional Lyrics*

2. Well, they'll stone ya when you're walkin' 'long the street.
   They'll stone ya when you're tryin' to keep your seat.
   They'll stone ya when you're walkin' on the floor.
   They'll stone ya when you're walkin' to the door.
   But I would not feel so all alone.
   Everybody must get stoned.

3. They'll stone ya when you're at the breakfast table.
   They'll stone ya when you are young and able.
   They'll stone ya when you're tryin' to make a buck.
   They'll stone ya and then they'll say, "Good luck."
   But I would not feel so all alone.
   Everybody must get stoned.

4. Well, they'll stone you and say that it's the end.
   Then they'll stone you and then they'll come back again.
   They'll stone you when you're riding in your car.
   They'll stone you when you're playing your guitar.
   Yes, but I would not feel so all alone.
   Everybody must get stoned.

5. Well, they'll stone you when you walk all alone.
   They'll stone you when you are walking home.
   They'll stone you and then say you are brave.
   They'll stone you when you're set down in your grave.
   But I would not feel so all alone.
   Everybody must get stoned.

# Shelter from the Storm

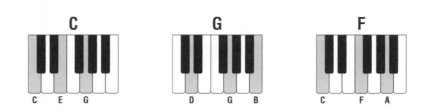

Words and Music by
Bob Dylan

Moderate half-time feel

1. 'Twas in an-oth-er life-time, one of toil and
2.–10. *(See additional lyrics)*

blood, when black-ness was a vir-ture and the

road was full of mud. I came in from the

wil - der - ness, a crea - ture void of form. "Come

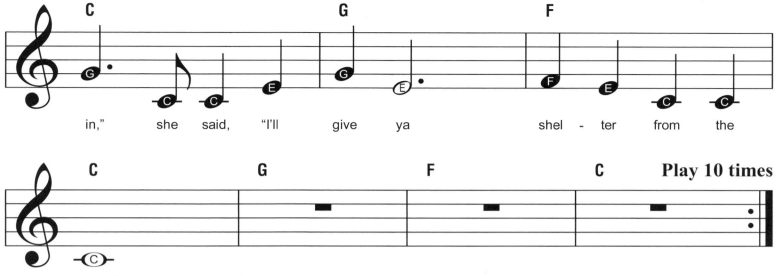

in," she said, "I'll give ya shel - ter from the

storm."

*Additional Lyrics*

2. And if I pass this way again, you can rest assured
   I'll always do my best for her; on that I give my word.
   In a world of steel-eyed death and men who are fighting to be warm,
   "Come in," she said, "I'll give ya shelter from the storm."

3. Not a word was spoke between us; there was little risk involved.
   Everything up to that point had been left unresolved.
   Try imagining a place where it's always safe and warm.
   "Come in," she said, "I'll give ya shelter from the storm."

4. I was burned out from exhaustion, buried in the hail,
   Poisoned in the bushes and blown out on the trail,
   Hunted like a crocodile, ravaged in the corn.
   "Come in," she said, "I'll give ya shelter from the storm."

5. Suddenly, I turned around and she was standin' there
   With silver bracelets on her wrists and flowers in her hair.
   She walked up to me so gracefully and took my crown of thorns.
   "Come in," she said, "I'll give ya shelter from the storm."

6. Now there's a wall between us; somethin' there's been lost.
   I took too much for granted; I got my signals crossed.
   Just to think that it all began on a non-eventful morn.
   "Come in," she said, "I'll give ya shelter from the storm."

7. Well, the deputy walks on hard nails and the preacher rides a mount,
   But nothing really matters much; it's doom alone that counts.
   And the one-eyed undertaker, he blows a futile horn.
   "Come in," she said, "I'll give ya shelter from the storm."

8. I've heard newborn babies wailin' like a mournin' dove
   And old men with broken teeth stranded without love.
   Do I understand your question, man? Is it hopeless and forlorn?
   "Come in," she said, "I'll give ya shelter from the storm."

9. In a little hilltop village, they gambled for my clothes.
   I bargained for salvation and she gave me a lethal dose.
   I offered up my innocence; I got repaid with scorn.
   "Come in," she said, "I'll give ya shelter from the storm."

10. Well, I'm livin' in a foreign country, but I'm bound to cross the line.
    Beauty walks a razor's edge; someday I'll make it mine.
    If I could only turn back the clock to when God and her were born.
    "Come in," she said, "I'll give ya shelter from the storm."

# Subterranean Homesick Blues

Words and Music by
Bob Dylan

Upbeat Blues-Rock

1. John-ny's in the base-ment mix-in' up the med-i-cine. I'm on the pave-ment
2.–4. (See additional lyrics)

think-in' a-bout the gov-ern-ment. The man in the trench-coat, badge out, laid-off,

says he's got a bad cough, wants to get it paid off. Look out, kid. It's

some-thin' you did. God knows when, but you're do-in' it a-gain. You bet-ter

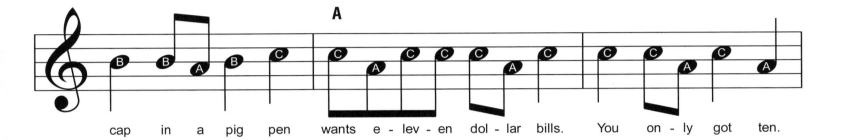

duck down the al - ley - way, look - in' for a new friend. The man in a coon - skin

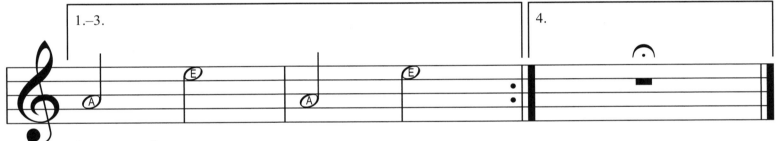

cap in a pig pen wants e - lev - en dol - lar bills. You on - ly got ten.

*(Instrumental)*

*Additional Lyrics*

2. Maggie comes fleet foot, face full of black soot,
   Talkin' that the heat put plants in the bed, but
   The phone's tapped anyway. Maggie says that many say
   They must bust in early May, orders from the D.A.
   Look out, kid. Don't matter what you did.
   Walk on your tiptoes, don't tie no bows.
   Better stay away from those that carry around a fire hose.
   Keep a clean nose, watch the plain clothes.
   You don't need a weatherman to know which way the wind blows.

3. Get sick, get well, hang around a ink well.
   Hang bail, hard to tell if anything is gonna to sell.
   Try hard, get barred, get back, write braille.
   Get jailed, jump bail, join the army if you fail.
   Look out, kid. You're gonna get hit.
   But losers, cheaters, six-time users hang around the theaters.
   Girl by the whirlpool is lookin' for a new fool.
   Don't follow leaders, watch the parkin' meters.

4. Get born, keep warm, short pants, romance, learn to dance.
   Get dressed, get blessed, try to be a success.
   Please her, please him, buy gifts, don't steal, don't lift.
   Twenty years of schoolin' and they put you on the day shift.
   Look out, kid. They keep it all hid.
   Better jump down a manhole, light yourself a candle.
   Don't wear sandals, try to avoid the scandals.
   Don't wanna be a bum, you better chew gum.
   The pump don't work 'cause the vandals took the handles.

# Tangled Up in Blue

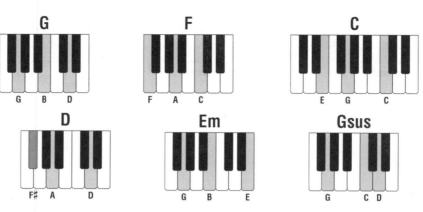

Words and Music by
Bob Dylan

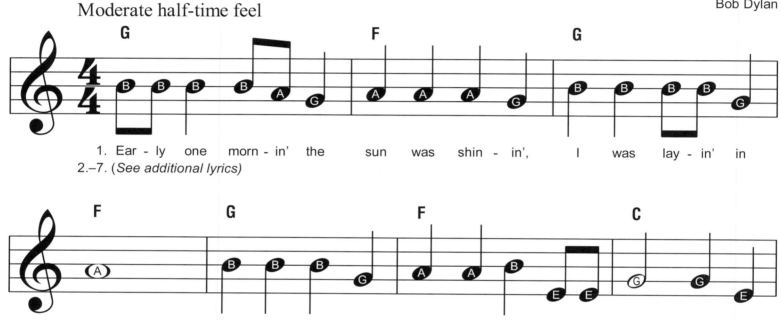

Moderate half-time feel

1. Ear - ly one morn - in' the sun was shin - in', I was lay - in' in
2.–7. (*See additional lyrics*)

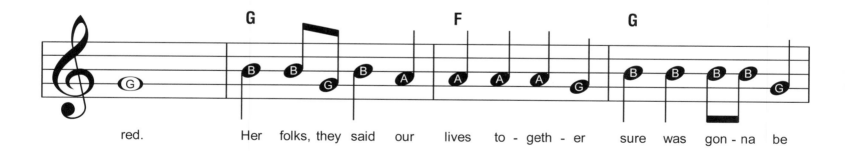

bed, won - d'rin' if she's changed at all, if her hair was still

red. Her folks, they said our lives to - geth - er sure was gon - na be

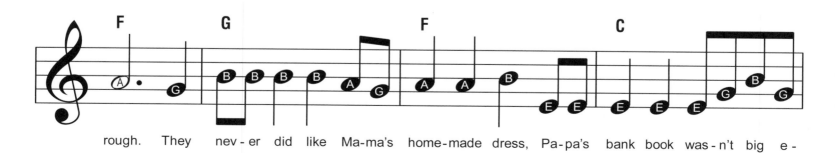

rough. They nev - er did like Ma - ma's home - made dress, Pa - pa's bank book was - n't big e -

nough. And I was stand - in' on the side of the road,

rain fall - in' on my shoes, head - ing out for the East Coast. Lord

knows I've paid some dues get - tin' through.

**Play 7 times**

Tan - gled up in blue.

*Additional Lyrics*

2. She was married when we first met,
Soon to be divorced.
I helped her out of a jam, I guess,
But I used a little too much force.
We drove that car as far as we could,
Abandoned it out West.
Split up on a dark, sad night,
Both agreeing it was best.
She turned around to look at me
As I was walkin' away.
I heard her say over my shoulder.
"We'll meet again someday on the avenue."
Tangled up in blue.

3. I had a job in the great north woods,
Working as a cook for a spell.
But I never did like it all that much,
And one day the ax just fell.
So I drifted down to New Orleans,
Where I lucky was to be employed,
Workin' for a while on a fishin' boat
Right outside of Delacroix.
But all the while I was alone,
The past was close behind.
I seen a lot of women,
But she never escaped my mind,
 and I just grew
Tangled up in blue.

4. She was workin' in a topless place,
And I stopped in for a beer.
I just kept lookin' at the side of her face
In the spotlight so clear.
And later on when the crowd thinned out,
I's just about to do the same.
She was standin' there in back of my chair,
Said to me, "Don't I know your name?"
I muttered somethin' underneath my breath,
She studied the lines on my face.
I must admit, I felt a little uneasy
When she bent down to tie the laces
 of my shoe.
Tangled up in blue.

5. She lit a burner on the stove
And offered me a pipe.
"I thought you'd never say hello," she said.
"You look like the silent type."
Then she opened up a book of poems
And handed it to me,
Written by an Italian poet
From the thirteenth century.
And every one of them words rang true
And glowed like burnin' coal,
Pourin' off of every page
Like it was written in my soul
 from me to you.
Tangled up in blue.

6. I lived with them on Montague Street
In a basement down the stairs.
There was music in the cafés at night
And revolution in the air.
Then he started into dealing with slaves,
And something inside of him died.
She had to sell everything she owned
And froze up inside.
And when finally the bottom fell out,
I became withdrawn.
The only thing I knew how to do
Was to keep on keepin' on like a bird that flew
Tangled up in blue.

7. So now I'm goin' back again;
I got to get to her somehow.
All the people we used to know,
They're an illusion to me now.
Some are mathematicians,
Some are carpenters' wives.
Don't know how it all got started,
I don't know what they're doin' with their lives.
But me, I'm still on the road,
Headin' for another joint.
We always did feel the same,
We just saw it from a different point of view.
Tangled up in blue.

# The Times They Are A-Changin'

Words and Music by
Bob Dylan

1. Come gath-er 'round, peo-ple, wher-ev-er you roam,
2.–5. (*See additional lyrics*)

___ and ad-mit that the wa-ters a-round you have

grown, and ac-cept it that soon you'll be drenched to the

bone. ___ If your time to you is worth

sav-in', ___ then you bet-ter start swim-min' or you'll

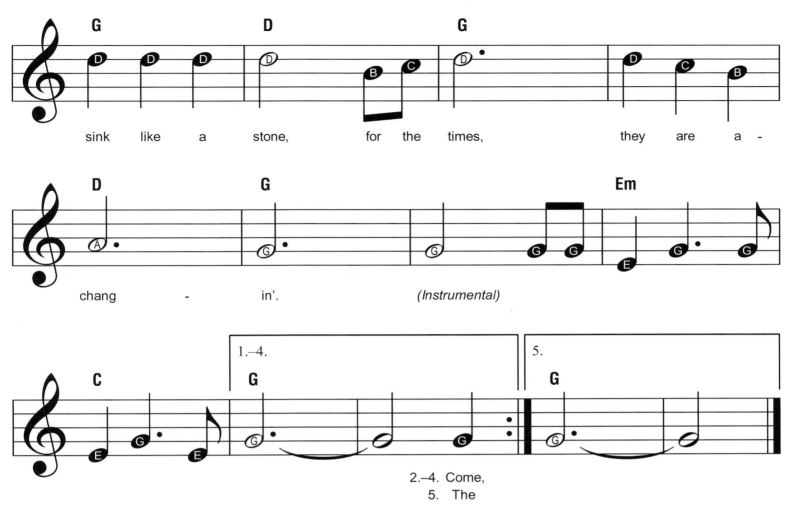

sink    like    a    stone,    for    the    times,    they    are    a -

chang    -    in'.    *(Instrumental)*

1.–4.    5.

2.–4. Come,
5.    The

*Additional Lyrics*

2. Come, writers and critics who prophesize with your pen,
And keep your eyes wide; the chance won't come again.
And don't speak too soon, for the wheel's still in spin,
And there's no tellin' who that it's namin'.
For the loser now will be later to win,
For the times, they are a-changin'.

3. Come, senators, congressmen; please heed the call.
Don't stand in the doorway, don't block up the hall.
For he that gets hurt will be he who has stalled.
The battle outside ragin'
Will soon shake your windows and rattle your walls,
For the times, they are a-changin'.

4. Come, mothers and fathers throughout the land,
And don't criticize what you can't understand.
Your sons and your daughters are beyond your command.
Your old road is rapidly agin'.
Please get out of the new one if you can't lend your hand,
For the times, they are a-changin'.

5. The line it is drawn, the curse it is cast.
The slow one now will later be fast.
As the present now will later be past,
The order is rapidly fadin'.
And the first one now will later be last,
For the times, they are a-changin'.

# SUPER EASY SONGBOOK

It's super easy! This series features accessible arrangements for piano, with simple right-hand melody, letter names inside each note, and basic left-hand chord diagrams. Perfect for players of all ages!

## THE BEATLES
00198161...............$14.99

## BEETHOVEN
00345533................$9.99

## BEST SONGS EVER
00329877...............$14.99

## BROADWAY
00193871...............$14.99

## JOHNNY CASH
00287524................$9.99

## CHRISTMAS CAROLS
00277955...............$14.99

## CHRISTMAS SONGS
00236850...............$14.99

## CLASSIC ROCK
00287526...............$14.99

## CLASSICAL
00194693...............$14.99

## COUNTRY
00285257...............$14.99

## DISNEY
00199558...............$14.99

## BILLIE EILISH
00346515...............$10.99

## FOUR CHORD SONGS
00249533...............$14.99

## FROZEN COLLECTION
00334069...............$10.99

## GEORGE GERSHWIN
00345536................$9.99

## GOSPEL
00285256...............$14.99

## HIT SONGS
00194367...............$14.99

## HYMNS
00194659...............$14.99

## JAZZ STANDARDS
00233687...............$14.99

## BILLY JOEL
00329996................$9.99

## ELTON JOHN
00298762................$9.99

## KIDS' SONGS
00198009...............$14.99

## LEAN ON ME
00350593................$9.99

## THE LION KING
00303511................$9.99

## ANDREW LLOYD WEBBER
00249580...............$14.99

## MOVIE SONGS
00233670...............$14.99

## POP SONGS FOR KIDS
00346809...............$14.99

## POP STANDARDS
00233770...............$14.99

## QUEEN
00294889................$9.99

## ED SHEERAN
00287525................$9.99

## SIMPLE SONGS
00329906...............$14.99

## STAR WARS
00345560................$9.99

## TAYLOR SWIFT
00323195................$9.99

## THREE CHORD SONGS
00249664...............$14.99

## TOP HITS
00300405................$9.99

Prices, contents and availability subject to change without notice.

Disney Characters and Artwork TM & © 2019 Disney

**HAL•LEONARD®**

www.halleonard.com